W9-BYL-604

*We're Finally Alone—*

## NOW WHAT DO WE DO?

# GREG JOHNSON

Tyndale House Publishers, Inc.
WHEATON, ILLINOIS

**Library of Congress Cataloging-in-Publication Data**

Johnson, Greg, date
  We're finally alone—   : now what do we do? / Greg Johnson.
    p.  cm.
  Includes bibliographical references and index.
  ISBN 0-8423-7848-0 (softcover : alk. paper)
  1. Marriage—Problems, exercises, etc.   2. Marriage—Religious aspects—Christianity.
3. Communication in marriage—Problems, exercises, etc.   4. Intimacy (Psychology)—
Problems, exercises, etc.  I. Title.

HQ734.J58   1996
646.7′8—dc20                                     95-40115

Printed in the United States of America

01  00  99  98  97  96  95
7    6   5   4   3   2   1

*We're Finally Alone—*

*Now What Do We Do?*

*To Elaine,*
*the bride of my youth.*

# Start Here!

Whether you are newly married or heading toward your twenty-fifth wedding anniversary, whether you're without children or your house is full of kids of all sizes, there are questions and exercises in this book especially for you.

Picture this: You've finally managed to carve out some "alone time." Perhaps you're at a restaurant, in the car, away on an overnighter, or maybe you're just lying in bed together with fifteen minutes of peace until you head off into dreamland.

It doesn't matter where you are—YOU'RE ALONE!

Now what?

That's the question my wife, Elaine, and I would think to ourselves whenever we finally got away from the kids. It's incredible to think how many times we would go out for dinner together, order our meal . . . then . . . then . . . sit and talk about the kids, the bills, the weather, work—but not the many other issues that were shaping our life together.

We've been married nearly twenty years, and both of us know that our relationship still needs a ton of investment, but we fall back into our old, predictable patterns of communication.

# *We're Finally Alone . . .*

It's safe.

Easy.

Nonthreatening—and too comfortable.

Comfort is good, but stagnation isn't. Have you ever seen a pond where water didn't come in and couldn't drain out?   If you have, you likely not only saw it, you smelled it! Stagnant waters smell. So do stagnant marriages.

What keeps a marriage moving? Free-flowing dialogue.

The key to a thriving marriage is not occasional great sex, cruises, meals out, or time away from the kids. It's the communication that occurs during those precious few moments when you can look into each other's eyes and attempt to reconnect.

That's what this book is all about—reconnecting, communicating, moving the waters.

## *How to Use This Book*

As you flip through the pages, you'll immediately notice that this book is divided into five "levels." Here's a quick explanation of what you'll find in each level.

**LEVEL ONE:** Fun, sometimes nonsense, a dip-your-toes-in-the-water: "I don't feel much like talking about anything too deep."

**LEVEL TWO:** A little more personal but still fairly light. You're saying to each other, "Let's take it a little bit deeper."

**LEVEL THREE:** You're getting to the self-revealing stage, but it shouldn't be anything too tough to handle if you're not fighting or mad at each other.

**LEVEL FOUR:** Both of you must be in the mood to answer questions and talk about issues that don't come up every day. Some could be uncomfortable, but if you're ready to take your marriage into deeper, more interesting waters, stay here awhile.

**LEVEL FIVE:** Intimacy anyone? At this level there are projects and sometimes (very) personal things to talk about. Once you're swimming out here, you'll discover things about your spouse you didn't know before.

When Elaine and I finally get alone long enough to connect, sometimes it's been a while. And though we're committed to intimacy, one of us will occasionally not want to work too hard to achieve it. That's OK. Most marriages go through these stages.

Other marriages may have one spouse realize—even desire—that the communication move into the deeper areas, but the other spouse may not be ready. Don't try to hurry your mate. Build one another's confidence in the shallow waters first; learn to trust each other before you take on the big waves. Be patient but persistent. Vitality and intimacy will come if you persevere.

# *We're Finally Alone . . .*

*Follow These Simple Principles of Fair and Honest Communication*

Talking about yourself or issues that are personal can sometimes get a bit . . . uncomfortable. Discomfort isn't justification for avoiding the issue. But there are right ways and wrong ways to talk; right ways help you make a genuine connection, and wrong ways throw up barriers of defense or silence. As you're going through this book together, keep these principles in mind.

1. When one person is talking, the other can't interrupt. If you need more explanation or have a question, agree on a signal: Twirl your finger, raise your hand, sneeze uncontrollably, put your pinky in your ear, pretend you're having a heart attack. Be dull or creative, but be courteous to one another.

2. If one person says, "That's too personal," or "I'm not ready for that one yet; can we go to another?" ask *once,* "Are you sure? I really want to know." But don't press. The goal isn't to make this book a one-shot experience. If you want your partner to say, "Hey, this is good stuff—fun, too," then take it at a pace both of you can manage.

3. When one of you says, "I feel . . . ," it is absolutely forbidden for the other to communicate (through words, looks, or body language), "Don't feel that way." Feelings are feelings. A better response is to say, "What can I do [about me or the situation] to help you *not* feel that way?"

4. If you notice your spouse is *very uncomfortable* (he or she is looking away, tries to change the subject, or actually leaves the room), drop it. But don't move onto the next one with the attitude, "Well, I guess you're not ready for this one. I'll make a note to get to it in two years when you've finally got some depth of character." Simply select something else. Yes, it's OK to make a mental note to try to bring it up again, but some things really *are* too painful or personal to talk about—even with a loving spouse.

5. No sarcasm. Words can be weapons, and sarcasm is often the weapon of choice because it is *seemingly* painless. Sarcasm has a sharp point. And it doesn't really help to say in your own defense, "I was just kidding." Usually sarcasm indicates that there's really some anger present.

6. Be aware of your nonverbal communication. It often makes the wrong statement—or it tells the truth when your words don't. Hold hands, make eye contact, and try to genuinely show your spouse that this time is important to you. If you're looking off in the distance or at the waitress/waiter walking by while you're spouse is really working at being a self-revealer, you're sending the wrong message. Pay attention!

7. Unless loudness is a strong trait of your ethnic origin or your spouse is hard of hearing, try not to raise your voice. That's a wall to intimacy that's tough to climb.

# We're Finally Alone . . .

## How to Go through This Book

Each question, quote, and project has a number attached to it. Instead of just starting at the beginning and going through the book (an option you could do if you want), we recommend you put a little fun into it. Simply call out a number, turn to it, read it, then answer it or do whatever it says. You know what you're ready to handle, so if you're not in the mood for a minor project or a deeper subject, don't pick a 400- or 500-level number. And if the question seems too dumb or easy, skip it.

Keep a pencil or pen handy to check off numbers you've completed. If both of you agree you'd like to talk about a certain subject, as opposed to going through the book haphazardly, use the index. Categories have been identified by number for your convenience. (No fair memorizing the index if you've got an agenda, though!)

What if you hit a number you're not ready to talk about? The two of you need to decide what your ground rules are. Maybe you could try this: If *you* call the number, you've got to answer it—no matter what. But if *your spouse* calls the number, you have the option of waiting until later. That way any "agenda" either of you has in mind won't be met. *The goal isn't merely to make your point, but to talk to and hear one another.*

This isn't a book to hurry through. The object isn't to "get done with it." The goal is to move to deeper levels of communication—and intimacy—one level, one caring conversation, at a time.

*100* What are the three best memories you have of us together before we were married?

    1. _____

    2. _____

    3. _____

*101* If you had to give up one of your five senses (sight, hearing, taste, touch, smell), which would you choose to live without?

*102* Describe the best teacher you ever had.

*103* If you suddenly won a million dollars, how would you spend it?

**104** List or describe five ways of showing affection that do not include kissing, hugging, holding hands, or sexual intercourse:

1. _____

2. _____

3. _____

4. _____

5. _____

**105** Do you believe each person has a guardian angel? What difference, if any, would it make to you if this were the case?

**106** Name a few of your all-time favorite movies; TV shows; songs; music groups.

**107** What's the most frightening thing that has ever happened to you?

**108** I appreciate it when you . . .

**109** What's your favorite hymn? favorite chorus? favorite camp song? Why are they favorites?

*110* What's the best prank you've ever played on someone? What's the best prank someone has ever played on *you?*

*111* What makes you laugh uncontrollably?

*112* Would you like it if I called you more often when we're apart, just for a brief chat?

*113* Why don't we give each other more back rubs?

*114* What's your favorite outdoor sport? indoor sport? group sport? individual sport?

*115* What one question will you be sure to ask God when you meet him?

*116* What are a few things I do for you that refresh you the most?

*117* Would you like to make love tonight or wait until the morning?

*118* Tell about the best vacation you've ever taken.

*119*  Are you an exaggerator? If so, why? When do you
tend to exaggerate the most?

*120*  Do you know my clothing sizes (shirt, top, pants,
dress, shoes, ring, hat)? What are my body
measurements (waist, hips, bust)?

*121*  Do you think we go straight to heaven or hell when
we die, or do we stay in our "dead" state until
Christ returns?

*122*  Who are your heroes or people you've looked up
to over the years?

*123*  If I hired a skywriter to put a message in the sky
about you, what do you think I would say?

*124*  What's a new Christmas tradition we could start
this year?

*125*  If you won an all-expense-paid trip to anywhere in
the world, where would you go?

*What one question*

*will you be sure*

*to ask God*

*when you meet him?*

**126** If you could write a book, what would you title it? What would it be about? How much would you sell it for?

**127** Describe all of my different voice tones and what I'm trying to communicate when I use them.

**128** What are your favorite comic strips in the newspaper and why? If you don't read them, why not?

**129** Do you secretly wish I'd cook more? Have you ever thought about our taking a cooking class together?

**130** Do you think that we generally get involved with people who are good for us and for our relationship to one another and to God? If there are questionable relationships, what should we do about them?

**131** Would you be willing to donate parts of your body to science after you die? How would you feel if your parents wanted *their* bodies donated to science?

132   Would you like to hold hands more often?

133   Are there any predictable things about me that you really like? How about some that really bug you?

134   Are you apathetic about anything these days? If so, what, and how do you get out of this frame of mind?

135   In what ways am I too careful? too careless?

136   In what areas should I feel more confident about myself?

137   If you could go back in time, what period of history would you choose? Why?

138   What outrages you the most about the world around you?

139   In what ways are we like night and day? Has this been good, bad, or not made a difference?

140  Try to think of three of your most embarrassing
     moments:

     1. _____

     2. _____

     3. _____

141  When do you feel most glad that you married me?

142  Do I honor you around the children? around others?

143  Do you have the ability to put the little things into
     perspective? What about the big things?

144  What impressed you most about me when we first
     started dating? How about now?

145  What were the slang words you used when you
     were a kid *(groovy, keen, neato, you dig)*?

146  When you set your mind to something, you
     are like . . .

*If you could write*

*a book, what would*

*you title it?*

*What would it be about?*

*How much would you*

*sell it for?*

*147* Do I ever send you mixed signals, confusing you about my motives or intentions? If so, in what area of our life together does this tend to happen?

*148* Am I ever too competitive? In what sports, games, or situations?

*149* When am I most cheerful? Should I be cheerful more often?

*150* What things in this world are worth dying for?

*151* Were you ever taught that sex was naughty?

*152* Do I ever act mean? What are your inner and outer responses when that happens?

*153* How did your parents discipline you through the years? Was it ever inappropriate? Was it too lax?

*154* How good were your parents at keeping their promises?

*155* Are we showing enough affection toward each other around the kids?

*156*  Do you ever wish I were more "artsy"?

*157*  When you didn't understand something in school, did you ask questions or remain quiet?

*158*  What really gets on your nerves?

*159*  Which makes you most uncomfortable while watching TV or movies: sex, violence, or bad language?

*160*  What new Easter tradition could we start this year?

*161*  Have you ever been to another country (or if not another country, then another city or another region of this country)? Which one? What differences between that place and home did you notice? Would you like to go back?

*162*  What was your curfew? How did you and your folks come up with it? Did you ever violate it, and, if so, what happened?

*163*  If there was one talent you could get for a wish, what would it be?

*164*  What is your favorite month of the year and why?

*165*  Do I use any pet names for you that you don't really like? Which ones *do* you like?

*166*  Would you describe yourself during your teenage years as capable of adapting easily to the people you were with or more concerned with being your own person?

*167*  What were your hobbies while you were growing up?

*168*  What did you like most about having brothers and sisters? What did you like least?
**or**
What did you like most about being an only child? What did you like least?

*169*  What is the best compliment I could give you?

*170*  Do I know how to express affection without having any sexual expectations? *(Hey, how did this tough one get in the Level One questions?)*

*171* Do I say "I love you" too much, too little, or often enough?

*172* Did you ever think it was possible to get an almost perfect spouse? When was that dream shattered?

*173* Am I ever irreverent? If so, how do you feel when I'm that way?

*174* What's the craziest thing you've ever done? Would you do it again?

*175* What city would you like us to spend a few days in—by ourselves—sightseeing?

*176* Tell about three of your weirdest (or worst) dates in high school or college.

*177* Am I generally an optimist or a pessimist? How do you feel about that?

*178* *A man's sex drive is similar to a drum solo, while a woman's is the same as a finely tuned orchestra.*[1]

Do you think this is a true statement? Why or why not?

*179* Does the statement "I told you so" ever come up in our relationship? If so, how can we eliminate it?

*180* Tell about three of your best dates in high school or college.

*181* How do you really feel about taking showers together?

*182* Do I show appreciation for the little things you do? How? How could I do that more often?

*183* How have you been affected by (choose the statement that applies to you):
• our having waited to have children?
• our becoming parents so early in our marriage?
• our not being able to have children of our own?

*184* Should we invest in a Do Not Disturb sign?

*185* Did you ever cheat on class assignments or tests? If so, were you ever caught? What happened?

*186* What comedians do you like most? Why?

*Do I show*

*appreciation for the*

*little things you do?*

*How?*

*How could I*

*do that more often?*

**187** How much TV do we watch in a week? Is it too much? What are three ways it affects us?

1. _____

2. _____

3. _____

Is there any way we should adjust or change this part of our time?

**188** Do I say please and thank you enough for the little and big things that you do?

**189** Can you think of a promise I made but didn't keep in the last six months? How did you feel about that?

**190** Were you ever called names by kids when you were growing up? How do you think that affected you? Were you ever called names by your parents? How do you think that affected you?

**191** When sex is "through" for me, do you ever think I leave you too quickly? How easy is it for you to say to me, "I'm not done yet"?

*192* Am I a sympathetic person? How can you tell?

*193* What subjects in school were easy for you, and which ones were tougher?

*194* How do you like to be pampered (when I'm in the mood to pamper you)?

*195* What could we do to exercise together on a regular basis?

*196* What would you think if I bought you some revealing or "creative" underwear once a year or so?

*197* Have you ever done anything particularly brave?

*198* When you're daydreaming, what things do you imagine yourself doing?

*199* Is there anyone you'd want to trade lives with? Who?

*200* Before we were married, were your closest friends girls or guys? Why?

*201* Is there a hobby you've always wanted to take up? How can you do that now?

*202* Do you think you spend most of your time doing what you are well suited to do? (This can be a job out of the home or activities in general.)

*203* What do you think your spiritual gifts are? How can you work at developing them, and how can I help you in this?

*204* Should we spend more time at separate functions, such as a women's retreat or a men's breakfast out? How could this benefit us?

*205*   What are the characteristics of a healthy church home? Have we found such a church yet?

*206*   If I had to leave the career I'm in, what other job or career could you see me entering successfully?

*207*   Are there issues we seem to have trouble discussing? Can we make a note of them and think about why they are difficult and what we might do to help us communicate about them?

*208*   What burdens (emotional, financial, spiritual) do we have now that we didn't have ten years ago? five years ago? last year? How can we adjust to them?

*209*   What kind of support systems should be part of any family (church family, close friends, professional contacts, medical help, counseling options, etc.)? How many of these are in place and operating well for us? If one of us were to get very ill or have to be away for an extended period of time, what kind of backup systems do we have for money? for help with the children? for anything else?

*If I had to leave*

*the career I'm in,*

*what other job*

*or career could*

*you see me entering*

*successfully?*

**210** *A good marriage would be between a blind wife and a deaf husband.*—MONTAIGNE, *Essays, III*[1]

To what degree is this true? false?

**211** Have you ever thought about "adopting" an elderly person in a nursing home or senior-citizen housing complex and including him or her in family activities and celebrations?

**212** What can (or what do) I say or do to help you feel sexy and attractive?

**213** What helps you grow closer to Christ? What things interfere with your spiritual life?

**214** Do you think there is anyone who looks up to you? How do you feel about being someone's role model?

**215** Is our marriage ever like two teams playing against each other?

**216** What would you like to do that we are unable to do now, due to lack of money, time, or ability? How can we dream together in that direction?

217　Do I spend enough of my free time with you? Are there other things that cut into our time together?

218　Talk about the top five best times you had with your mom and dad.

219　Do you believe the Rapture (when Christians are taken to heaven) will occur before, during, or after the Tribulation?

220　What do you not understand about the Bible that you'd like to ask someone about? Have you asked anyone? Who do you think would have the answer to this question?

221　Do you think it's OK to "pull the plug" on someone who's terminally ill and wants to die?

222　When was the last time you got so angry you could hardly control yourself? How do you normally handle your anger?

223　Was it easy to tell your parents you loved them? How often did they say it to you?

*224*    Every couple should know how to save pleasant thoughts and good memories as much as money.[2]

How can we start a "bank account" of these things so we don't forget them?

*225*    Why is it so uncomfortable for the average couple to talk about sex? Do you feel a need to talk about it more?

*226*    Do you ever find yourself getting jealous of others because of the talents they have?

*227*    How do you feel when you're around someone who is honest about his or her shortcomings?

*228*    Have we learned any hard lessons in the last six months? If so, what are they?

*229*    What did you like most about being a teenager?

*230*    Of everything you've done, what makes you feel most proud?

*Was it easy*

*to tell your parents*

*you loved them?*

*How often did they*

*say it to you?*

**231** What do you think about tracking our expenses or starting a budget? When could we do that?

**232** What do you enjoy most about your life? What would you like to change?

**233** Describe an instance when someone really let you down. How did you feel? Were you able to forgive, or is it still an issue for you?

**234** Do you like it when people are brutally honest with you? Do you like to be brutally honest with other people?

**235** Are you happy with the way you handle compliments?

**236** Do I say "I love you" often enough?

**237** What words or actions on my part throughout the day or week really set the stage for a great time of lovemaking?

**238** Do you ever wish I were more spontaneous or more structured? In what ways?

239 What could I do in public that would embarrass or hurt you? Have I ever done something like this?

240 Does it ever seem that I'm not giving you my full attention when you're talking to me?

241 What are some little things in life that we sometimes take for granted?

242 Do you believe that God performs miracles today? In what ways? When was the last time a miracle happened to us?

243 What do you think about camping out in the backyard and making love under the stars after the kids are in bed?

244 In what ways is our marriage a good example for our children?

245 How good are you at saying no to things that would rob you of time as a couple? (Think about commitments you make and those that are made for your children.)

*246* How do you respond to feelings of guilt?

*247* Do you ever feel that my compliments are hollow? If so, when is this the case, and why do you think I'm being insincere?

*248* What types of little gifts go a long way toward showing you how much I'm thinking about you?

*249* Did you want your spouse to be smarter and more attractive than you? less intelligent and less attractive? Explain your reasoning.

*250* Do you believe it's important for Christians to take Communion? What does taking Communion mean to you?

*251* If you could change anything about the way you look or act, what would it be?

*252* What do you learn just by watching people?

*253* Share three things about your grade school years you have never told me.

*In what ways*

*is our marriage*

*a good example*

*for our children?*

*254*  Share three things about your junior high years you have never told me.

*255*  Did you ever see your mom or dad express deep emotion? How did you feel when this happened?

*256*  What's the difference between happiness and joy?

*257*  Name five things I could do that would pleasantly surprise you:

1. _____

2. _____

3. _____

4. _____

5. _____

*258*  What do you want written on your tombstone? (Pretend you'll have one.)

*259*  If you could know the future—but not have the power to change it—would you want to know it?

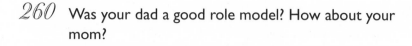

260   Was your dad a good role model? How about your mom?

261   Name five things you have always been able to count on me for:

     1. _____

     2. _____

     3. _____

     4. _____

     5. _____

262   Do I sometimes make a joke out of things you don't think are funny? How much does that really bother you? Would you like me to change?

263   How does it make you feel when we sometimes have to agree to disagree? Is this a good way to settle things?

264   What things used to embarrass you a lot? How about now?

265 What are the top five best ways to give you a tangible expression of my love?

    1. _____

    2. _____

    3. _____

    4. _____

    5. _____

266 If you could meet anyone in the Bible (besides Jesus), who would it be, and why?

267 Think back to a time when you did something stupid or embarrassing. How did you react? Do you tend to act as if such incidents are no big deal? Do you direct attention to someone else in self-defense? Do you laugh at yourself and put others at ease?

268 What did your parents believe about alcohol? gambling?

269 Do you believe being involved in church is important? What do you like most about our church?

270 What would you rather have had from your mom and dad: more gifts or more time?

271 What can we do to grab fifteen minutes a day of uninterrupted talk when we're both awake enough to pay attention?

272 If you try and fail at something, are you less likely to try it again, or does it make you want to succeed at it all the more? Can you give any examples?

273 What used to be most important to you: looks, talent, or brains?

274 How well did your parents communicate? Was one "the talker" and one more quiet?

275 Do I ever exaggerate? Are such habits frustrating to you, or do you tend to take them in stride?

276 What do you think about God's judgment? What are you most fearful of?

277 What are a few things your parents were right about after all?

*278*   How important is it for us to teach patriotism to our children? How can we do that better?

*279*   How can I best express love to your mother and father? Are there areas in which I'm in a better position than you are (i.e., I'm not their child) to support or help them? How would you like to see me improve in my relationship to members of your family?

*280*   In what type of setting have you always wanted to make love?

*281*   What type of conscience do you have?
(a) overactive
(b) buried
(c) scarred
(d) just right

*282*   What do you think we could do to give our kids a more well-developed, but balanced, conscience?

*283*   Do we need another couple who could help our marriage grow through their friendship and experience?

284 Should we consider befriending a younger couple to see if God would want us to be mentors in their lives?

285 What are five things that you perceive I get *really* excited about?

1. _____

2. _____

3. _____

4. _____

5. _____

286 When we argue, is it about little things or big things? How do you feel about that?

287 *You should remember that though another may have more money, beauty, and brains than you, yet when it comes to the rarer spiritual values such as charity, self-sacrifice, honor, nobility of heart, you have an equal chance with everyone to be the most beloved and honored of all people.*—ARCHIBALD RUTLEDGE[3]

Since example is the best way to teach this to our children, how would our time priorities have to change to begin living these types of attitudes?

**288** Do I praise you enough in front of others? How do you feel when I do this?

**289** How do you handle your own mistakes?
  (a) accept the blame and try to learn from what's happened
  (b) deflect the blame to others
  (c) try to ignore the issue
  (d) get depressed and think of yourself as a failure

**290** What are a few things your parents were wrong about after all?

**291** What were your fears when you were a kid? How about now?

**292** What's the difference between encouraging someone and complimenting someone?

**293** *I am not a teacher, but an awakener.*—ROBERT FROST

In what ways can we do this more with our children? with each other?

"I AM NOT A TEACHER,
BUT AN AWAKENER."
ROBERT FROST

*In what ways*

*can we do this more*

*with our children?*

*with each other?*

**294** What three things could we do in the next six months to help us live on less than our paychecks?

1. _____

2. _____

3. _____

**295** Do you think it's important to invite people to church? Do you feel comfortable doing so?

**296** TO THE WIFE: In what ways is your husband still a little boy? (Is this good or bad?)
TO THE HUSBAND: In what ways is your wife still a little girl? (Is this good or bad?)

**297** As a childless couple, what can we offer to our church and community?
**or**
As parents, what can we offer to our church and community?

**298** Are there friends or relatives for whom you've grown weary of praying that they come to know Christ? If so, who are they?

*299* Doug Fields says that "positive memories can become anchors for future storms."[4] Are we creating enough good memories for and with each other to make the tough times bearable? What can we do to start creating more?

300  When are the times you feel like escaping and just taking a hot bath with no interruptions?

301  What first attracted you to me? Is attraction still important?

302  What do you think makes a brave man? a brave woman?

303  Are we being consistent in our discipline with each of our children?

304  If you could spend a whole day by yourself, what would you do? How often do you need that type of privacy?

305  Have I ever been a faultfinder with you or the kids? What are some ways I could be more encouraging?

*306* What, if anything, are you most cynical about?

*307* What kinds of activities do you wish we would do more often as a family (having meals together, playing, traveling, etc.)?

*308* Are you satisfied with how I make decisions about what to buy and what bills to pay?

*309* What would you say if I told you I wanted to have more kids?

*310* What have our children (or other children in our extended family) added to our lives?

*311* Do you think we are involved enough in ministry that affects our community and the social needs we see around us? What steps might we take to be better informed or more involved?

*312* Is sex helpful, comforting, difficult, or anxiety producing for you when you are under stress at work? grieving? sad? How can our intimacy at those times be at its best?

*313* When was the last time you cried? Why?

*314* Do I hug you enough?

*315* If we were to read a book together, what kind would it be? Do you have any suggestions? How could we make the time?

*316* When you were an adolescent, how important to you was being popular? To what extent did you notice friends at school trying to be popular?

*317* In what areas do we minister to others better as a team? In what areas are we better ministers as individuals?

*318* Which one of us initiates sex most often? Are you happy with it that way, or do you think we should make a change?

*319* What sport or hobby could we take up together?

*320* How often do you really think about me each day? What do those thoughts consist of?

**321** What do you think it means to be "called" by God to do a certain task or fill a particular function? Have you ever been convinced that you were called to a ministry or job?

**322** What kind of gifts do you appreciate most from me: bought or handmade ones?

**323** TO THE HUSBAND: How do you feel when you see and hear your wife crying?
TO THE WIFE: What goes through your mind when you see your husband cry?

**324** What do you think it means to be spiritually blind? At what times or in what ways do you think you are spiritually blind?

**325** Do you think we are financially secure? If not, what seems insecure about our situation? What might we do to remedy that?

**326** When do you judge yourself the most harshly? How should I respond when that happens? Do I ever judge you harshly? If so, in what situations?

*In what areas
do we minister to others
better as a team?
In what areas
are we better ministers
as individuals?*

327 *Faith is not belief without proof, but trust without reservations.*—ELTON TRUEBLOOD[1]

Do you trust God without reservations? If you have some, what are they?

328 Do I forgive you by my actions as well as my words?

329 Talk about how your relationship with your in-laws could be improved.

330 Start to think about how you want to celebrate your 10th, 20th, 25th, etc. anniversary together. Make big plans, then start working toward that goal (perhaps opening a separate savings account for it).

331 *Happiness comes of the capacity to feel deeply, to enjoy simply, to think freely, to risk life, to be needed.*—STORM JAMESON[2]

What do you think of this quote? How is it working out in our marriage?

332 FROM THE WIFE: When I'm at the worst time in my cycle, the best things you can do are . . .

333 What distracts you from pursuing me romantically?

334 Does anything frighten you about the future?

335 At what times do you get that overwhelmed feeling? How do your body, emotions, and spirit react when that feeling hits?

336 "Sex is a drive, not a need." Do you agree with that statement? Why or why not?

337 When your parents leave this earth, how do picture yourself responding? If either has *already* left the earth, how did you react?

338 Talk about little ways you can "escape" from the kids on a weekly basis. It doesn't have to be a formal date; you don't even have to leave the house. But a creative way to get thirty minutes for just the two of you while your brain waves are still active could provide the lift your relationship needs (you could even take this book along with you!).

339 Is there anything about me that you have given up on trying to change?

**340** Do you wish you had the power to change me in some ways? Is this a worthy goal?

**341** Have you ever been so bummed-out on life that you wanted to run away? What did you do, or how did you get out of that mood?

**342** What do you think it means to "honor one another above yourselves" (Romans 12:10)?

**343** How am I helping or hindering you in reaching your potential? In what specific ways could I help?

**344** *To see her is to love her,*
*And love but her forever;*
*For nature made her what she is,*
*And ne'er made sic anither!*
—ROBERT BURNS, *O, Saw Ye Bonnie Lesley*[3]

God made only one you—and he made you for me. Even with that knowledge, people sometimes act as if they don't like the person God crafted so carefully. What can I do to help convince you that God didn't make any mistakes when he made you?

*345* Share three things about your high school years you have never told me.

*346* Share three things about your college years you have never told me.

*347* What does the thought of having (or getting) noticeable wrinkles do to you?

*348* What one thing that I do for you makes you feel truly loved and cared for?

*349* What do you think disappoints your parents most about you—even today? How do you feel about that?

*350* What things in life have eternal value?

*351* What do you remember most about our honeymoon? (Besides that!)

*352* Do you ever think about death? What do you think heaven and hell will be like?

**353** How has your devotional time with God been during the past month? Is there anything I can do to better support you in your faith life?

**354** Do you ever feel anxious about making love? If so, when and why?

**355** Describe some dream accomplishments for yourself at ages forty, sixty-five, and eighty.

**356** Do I try to defend myself too much? When I get defensive, how does that make you react?

**357** *Don't flatter yourself that friendship authorizes you to say disagreeable things to your intimates. The nearer you come into relation with a person, the more necessary do tact and courtesy become.*—OLIVER WENDELL HOLMES[5]

Does it seem that I've become less concerned with courtesy and tact since developing a marital friendship with you? Do I tend to do anything in the name of "being myself" that annoys or bothers you?

**358** How can we have more tact in the way we treat each other?

*Describe some dream accomplishments for yourself at ages forty, sixty-five, and eighty.*

**359**  *The silent treatment was invented by a kindergartner.*[4]

Do we ever give each other the silent treatment? If so, how do you feel when I do this? How might we break this pattern?

**360**  Have you ever attended a funeral? If so, what was that experience like for you?

**361**  What do you like best about being a parent? What do you like least?

**362**  What part of my body do you find most sexy? What behavior do you find most sexy?

**363**  What would happen to the kids if both of us died? Do we have everything in order so that there isn't a lot of trouble or confusion about money, custody, and so forth?

**364**  When we have a fight or an intense discussion, does it seem like I'm really listening to what you say, or am I more interested in getting in what I want to say? What signal can I give to let you know I'm listening and understanding what you're saying?

*365* What types of gifts could you give your parents that they would treasure for the rest of their lives?

*366* What experiences have you had that allow you to believe in a kind and loving God? Is there anything in the world that causes you to doubt this?

*367* Would you like to make love tonight or tomorrow morning?

*368* Do you say what people want to hear or what you really think? Are there times when you switch strategies?

*369* Do you think ambition is good or bad? Do I have too much? too little? about the right amount?

*370* What three things do you think I should be most ambitious about?

1. _____

2. _____

3. _____

*371*  In what ways are you like your mom? your dad?

*372*  When and with whom is it most difficult for you to be bold about your faith?

*373*  Have I ever done anything to "crush your spirit" (demotivate; take the wind out of your sails; put your emotions on hold; make you wonder if I'm the same person you married)?

*374*  How can I best help you deal with the occasional fears you have about the present or the future?

*375*  Have you ever thought about going into full-time ministry?

*376*  The best ways to remind me to pray for you and our family more often are . . .

*377*  Do you feel I ignore problems or face them head-on?

*378*  Do I act as though your opinions are important?

*379*  How do I go about solving problems? How could I improve my problem-solving skills?

380 If we started taking more walks together, what would be the potential pitfalls? the potential benefits?

381 What gifts do you think God has given you for serving him?

382 What do you think a healthy marriage looks like?

383 Do you ever sense that I sometimes put conditions on my love and affection for you? When do you feel the most insecure about my love?

384 Is there anything I do to excess? If so, how can I become more balanced in this area?

385 If divorce was never part of God's plan, why do you think so many Christian marriages end that way?

386 I would feel safer sharing my feelings with you if . . .

387 How can we set the right atmosphere in our marriage so that both of us feel safe sharing secrets and feelings with each other?

388  What does it mean to "work on" a marriage?

389  "Why do you look at the speck of sawdust in your brother's eye and pay no attention to the plank in your own eye?" (Matthew 7:3).

Do either of us have a tendency to point out the problems of the other without recognizing our own? How can we help each other live by a more Christlike pattern?

390  Do you think we could be more imaginative in the area of sexual expression? Do you have any suggestions or ideas?

391  What can we do to serve God by serving others together as a couple? as a family?

392  Who are your closest friends and why?

393  Describe your perfect date.

394  Do you believe in fate, luck, happenstance, or God's control in *every* circumstance? Why?

*Do you ever sense that I sometimes put conditions on my love and affection for you? When do you feel the most insecure about my love?*

395 Am I vulnerable enough with you, or does it seem like I'm holding a lot back that you should know about my life and emotions?

396 As we grow older together, in what ways do you love me more?

397 Am I consistent in matching my loving words toward you with loving behavior?

398 If I were to write more notes to you, what kinds of things would you like the notes to say?

399 What item in our schedule would you most like to change?

*400*   When you try something and fail, how do I respond? Is that what you really need?

*401*   Most marriages have some good things going for them. Among our married friends, what are some of the good things you would like to emulate?

*402*   If you could go back to school and take some classes, what would you like to take? What is holding you back? Is this a goal I should start helping you attain?

*403*   Do you think our level of alcohol consumption/ junk-food eating/TV watching might be influencing our children's viewpoint on the issue?

*404*   In what ways do I treat you like a fellow heir in Christ? In what ways don't I?

*405* What do you think it means that a good marriage is the best gift we can give our children?

*406* What is the best gift we can give our grandchildren?

*407* If I sometimes talked too much, would you be able to tell me that? Have I demonstrated before that I hear such messages?

*408* How do you think we demonstrate in marriage that we are a brother and sister in Christ? How can we do better at this?

*409* What do you think it takes to make and keep friends? Do you think you are good at this?

*410* Do you remember the wonder, the thankfulness, and the joy we had when our children were born? What would it take for us to feel that way more often about our kids today?

*411* What do you think our children need most from us: our presence at all times or a healthy marriage? *(And, no, you can't say both.)*

412 How you greet and say good-bye to each other says a lot about the level of affection in your relationship. Talk about the hellos and good-byes between you and what you like or dislike about them.

413 Many people discipline their children in the same way they were disciplined. Most of the time, do we agree on the reason for and the method of discipline? What should we do when we disagree?

414 Am I the type who always has to win, or am I skilled at compromise when it's necessary?

415 What gives you the motivation to get up in the morning? Do I help or hinder your "zest for living"?

416 When we're in the middle of making love, what things have you had the urge to tell me?

417 "A gentle answer turns away wrath, but a harsh word stirs up anger" (Proverbs 15:1).

Do I practice the first half of this proverb or the second?

418  Do you ever feel that I'm abdicating my role as a disciplinarian and leaving the "bad guy" role to you?

419  Do I act as if I'm content with our situation in life (job, health, finances)? How do my responses to life make you feel?

420  *The church exists to train its members through the practice of the presence of God to be servants of others, to the end that Christlikeness may become common property.*—WILLIAM ADAMS BROWN[1]

Is our church doing that for us and our children? What can we do to help it accomplish that goal?

421  *He has the right to criticize who has the heart to help.*—ABRAHAM LINCOLN[2]

Do I ever criticize you or the kids without offering a way to make things better?

422  When do you notice that I am/have been most insecure? When you are feeling insecure, what one thing helps strengthen you most of all?

**423** It's normal to occasionally feel "trapped" in marriage. Has there ever been a time when you've felt this way in our marriage? What is usually going on to make you feel this way?

**424** *Be not angry that you cannot make others as you wish them to be, since you cannot make yourself as you wish to be.*—THOMAS À KEMPIS[3]

Do you ever feel that my expectations for you are higher than they are for myself?

**425** How do I bring out your natural talents and abilities? Do I ever suppress them, and, if so, how? Should I be doing anything differently?

**426** What does the word *vulnerable* mean to you? Am I vulnerable? Should that be a goal in our relationship?

**427** Is there any emotional "baggage" we've brought into this marriage that needs to be unpacked? Do you think this process requires professional help, or can we handle it ourselves?

428 Have we had sexual difficulties to the point that you think some outside help—books, counseling, or a talk with our physician—would be helpful?

429 Do you remember any time when you were going to "lose it" with one of the kids? What could have I done—or what could have been done—to prevent it?

430 Talk about the best ways you've developed for "clearing the air" in your relationship.

431 Have you ever felt that one of us is taking on an unfair measure of responsibility in our home (for finances, for emotional stability, for household matters, for parenting, for faith, etc.)? If so, is this a consistent problem, or do responsibilities seem to shift only at certain times?

432 What does verbal affection mean to you? Do we give each other enough verbal affection? How can we strengthen this aspect of our communication?

433 In terms of honesty, how would you characterize
our relationship? (Circle and talk about all that apply.
(a) Don't ask, don't tell.
(b) I am totally honest about the small stuff.
(c) I am totally honest about everything.
(d) I know you hide a few things, but I deal with this
approach better than knowing all the truth.
(e) I'm afraid to tell you some things sometimes for
fear of how you'll respond.
(f) I don't talk because I feel that you can't handle
the truth.
(g) Other

434 Do you ever have doubts about God's character,
about the Bible, or about Jesus—if he is actually
who he said he was? How do you express these
doubts?

435 Are you ever envious of what others have or what
others are doing with their lives?

436 What are your beliefs as to why there is suffering
and death in the world? Do you think your beliefs
would change if we had to deal with major suffering
or death on a more personal level?

437 What "ruts," if any, has your marriage fallen into in the past? How about today? Talk about how you can work your way out of the ones both of you don't like.

438 "God saw all that he had made, and it was very good" (Genesis 1:31).

God had created male and female, including their emotional and sexual differences. "It was very good" is what Scripture concludes. Are you as a couple able to say the same thing about your emotional and sexual differences?

439 Have either of you ever felt that you were the only one in this marriage really trying to make it work? It's common for one marriage partner to slack off for a short season, but when that happens for an extended period of time, bad habits start to form. Talk through renewing your commitment to work hard at making the relationship strong. How would you both have to change?

Are you ever envious

of what others have

or what others

are doing

with their lives?

*440* Think up a new tradition you can start together, something in which just the two of you would participate. It doesn't matter if it's yearly, quarterly, or monthly, just something both of you could look forward to. Here are a few suggestions to get you started:

- Have a yearly planning day or weekend at a nice place.
- Set the alarm and make love at midnight at every full moon (or no moon, or half-moon).
- Find a hole-in-the-wall restaurant where you can eat regularly; some place where you call the owner or waitress by name (and they know yours).
- Take a once-a-month Saturday drive to a nearby small town you've never been to and hit all of the antique shops, flea markets, and garage sales you can find.

*441* Since conflict is inevitable in marriage, knowing how to solve it is essential. In what ways have you tried to resolve conflicts in the past? Which one(s) worked best? Predict a potential conflict and decide how it could best be solved.

442 *I have held many things in my hands, and I have lost them all; but whatever I have placed in God's hands, that I still possess.*—MARTIN LUTHER[4]

In what specific ways are we living this statement? How can we live this truth even more?

443 Do I tend to make everything an issue or am I pretty good at majoring on the majors and minoring on the minors?

444 What have you learned about yourself through being a parent? What have you learned about me as you've watched me be a parent?

445 In what three ways can we enjoy each other more?

1. _____

2. _____

3. _____

446 Do you ever think about your own mortality? How do you "measure your days" without dwelling on death?

**447** *Doing little things with a strong desire to please God makes them really great.*—ST. FRANCIS DE SALES[5]

The small, mundane things in life that couples do for one another and their families are the things most people grow to resent, even loathe, while they're doing them. How can we turn the corner and realize those little things are actually times when we can please God?

**448** What do you think the phrase "emotional divorce" means? Have you known people who have gone through this? How do you think they got that way? Is there anything we need to talk about to keep us from heading in that direction?

**449** Without your spouse looking, write down three ways you can become a better listener.

1. _____

2. _____

3. _____

Next, write down three ways your mate can become a better listener.

1. _____

2. _____

3. _____

Compare notes.

*450* When do you feel the most distant from me? Does that feeling cause you to want to draw closer, move farther away, or stay where you are until the feeling goes away?

*451* *The first general rule for friendship is to be a friend, to be open, natural, interested; the second rule is to take time for friendship. Friendship, after all, is what life is finally about. Everything material and professional exists in the end for persons.*—NELS F. S. FERRE[6]

What parts of this quote fit me as a friend to you? Am I open, natural, interested in you? Do I take time to just be your friend, or do you sometimes sense another agenda?

452 Do I ever try to play God in your life, or do I encourage you to take that role in mine? Why would we do this, and how might we change our approach?

453 When we disagree on things, do I ever attack your character to win the argument instead of discussing the real issue?

454 What would you think if we started to have weekly meetings to talk through our schedule, the kids, the bills, the future, etc.? What day and time would be best for this?

455 *All that is essential for the triumph of evil is that good men do nothing.*—EDMUND BURKE[7]

Improving a marriage is work, but many couples do nothing but exist under the same roof and then expect their marriage to grow. Have you ever fallen into that trap as a couple? If so, what happened? What might happen in such a situation?

*456* We are put here to grow, and we ought to grow, and to use all the means of growth according to the laws of our being. The only real satisfaction there is, is to be growing up inwardly all the time, becoming more just, true, generous, simple, manly, womanly, kind, active. And this can we all do, by doing each day the day's work as well as we can.—JAMES FREEMAN CLARKE[8]

What in this quote do you agree or disagree with? Do you feel you are accomplishing the goal of doing each day's work as well as you can?

*457* In what ways do our children sometimes set the agenda for our marriage?

*458* Does my ego ever get in the way of your ability to love and respect me?

*459* If we were having a rough go of it over a long period (two months to a year), would you ever consider counseling to help set things right? What are your general feelings about third-party involvement when marriage hits a long-term rocky point?

*460*  What were your top three expectations of marriage before we were married?

1. _____

2. _____

3. _____

*461*  Are you ever tempted to compare me with past girlfriends/boyfriends, or with coworkers or acquaintances of the opposite sex? Are these fleeting thoughts, or do they sometimes take root?

*462*  *Grow old along with me!*
*The best is yet to be,*
*The last of life, for which the first was made.*
*Our times are in his hand*
*Who saith, "A whole I planned,*
*Youth shows but half; trust God:*
*see all nor be afraid!"*
—ROBERT BROWNING[9]

In what ways do you look forward to growing old together? In what ways does that prospect not look so fun?

463 Do I sometimes make you feel as if you have to work or perform to get my approval? How do I do that?

464 What three things can we start doing to become better friends?

1. _____

2. _____

3. _____

465 What does it mean to you to have a good self-image? What do you think of yourself . . . really?

466 What does being contented mean to you? Do you ever feel that way? When?

467 TO THE WIFE: What is it about female friendships that sometimes make them deeper than marriage friendships?
TO THE HUSBAND: Why do friendships between men seem more superficial than those between women? Do you think that males in general have the capacity to be friends with very many people?

**468** What are some of the most important lessons about life you've learned this past year?

**469** In some ways, marriage is like a team relationship. In the area of bringing up our children, how well are we doing as teammates?

**470** *True generosity requires more of us than kindly impulse. Above all it requires imagination—the capacity to see people in all their perplexities and needs, and to know how to expend ourselves effectively for them.*
—I. A. R. WYLIE[10]

In what ways am I imaginative when it comes to giving myself to others in big or small ways? How could I be more perceptive when it comes to being generous toward you?

**471** As soon as you get near your calendar, plan . . .
• the next time you have lunch together
• your next Friday or Saturday night date
• your next night alone together
• your next weekend alone together

*What are some of the most important lessons about life you've learned this past year?*

472  Have you ever fasted on a regular basis in order to get closer to God? What do you know about fasting? What do you think about fasting once a month or once a week together (even if it were just for one meal a day)?

473  The best way to say no to my intention or request for sex is . . .

474  How do you really feel about making an "appointment" for sex?

475  Whose responsibility is it to keep up the courtship in our marriage? In what ways could I "court" you more?

476  TO THE WIFE: What three things does your husband do that really make you feel like a woman? TO THE HUSBAND: What three things does your wife do that really make you feel like a man?

477  Next time you're near the yellow pages, pick out one museum that you'd like to stroll through together. Then, set a day on the calendar when you can go (with or without kids—but preferably without).

**478** Do I have a tendency to deal immediately with little "weeds" (minor irritations) in our marriage, or do I wait until they become more of a "hedge" (something that temporarily comes between us)?

**479** If I were to die suddenly next week, what little things would you miss about me the most?

**480** How do you really feel about my parents (or stepparents)?

**481** What is one pet peeve you have about something I do that you've never mentioned before? On a scale of 1 to 10, how big of a deal is it?

**482** What do you think "marital intimacy" means?

**483** What do you enjoy most when we make love? least?

**484** *With all thy faults, I love thee still.*
—WILLIAM COWPER, *The Task*, II[11]

What faults do I have that you have easily overlooked through the years? Which ones are sometimes more difficult to overlook today?

**485** Do you ever feel that I intentionally hide from you instead of engaging in meaningful discussions or fun times together? How about unintentionally? What can we do to solve this?

**486** *Doubt thou the stars are fire;*
*Doubt that the sun doth move;*
*Doubt truth to be a liar;*
*But never doubt I love.*
—SHAKESPEARE, *Hamlet, II, 2*[12]

What today—in any way—makes you doubt that my love for you is growing deeper, expanding wider, and becoming more real than it was last year?

**487** In your opinion, what sets me off in a fit of anger more than anything else? When that happens, what do you feel like doing or saying?

**488** Can you be a jealous person? What can make you jealous?

**489** This is a tough one: Do you ever use sex as a reward? Have you ever withheld affection or sexual activity in order to punish me or get me to do what you wanted?

490 In what five ways can I inspire you to do and be
your best?

1. _____

2. _____

3. _____

4. _____

5. _____

491 How would you feel if all God asked you to do in
life was bring up your children to love and obey
Jesus Christ—if you never became rich or famous,
but were "ordinary"? Though you worked hard and
served others when you could, but didn't leave a
legacy that hundreds (in your life) would praise you
for . . . would you have lived a life worth living?

492 What would be the worst thing that could happen
to our family? How could our marriage survive as
well as thrive through it?

493 What causes the most chronic stress in our
marriage (work, finances, children, health, marriage
relationship itself, other)? How can we work
together to handle this?

494 List the gifts and talents you see in each of your children. Spend some time praying for the development of those gifts and talents. Brainstorm about how you, as parents, can be part of that process.

495 Are there times you feel lonely though we're sitting in the same room together?

496 How can we put more fun in our family?

497 What do you think it means to age gracefully? How are we doing?

498 When I disagree with you, how can I best communicate that without making you feel stupid? (Do I ever do that?)

499 Do you agree with the saying "Absence makes the heart grow fonder"? Do you think this statement applies to us?

*What do you
think it means
to age gracefully?
How are we doing?*

500    Constructive criticism is sometimes tough to give a spouse—yet it is often necessary in order to help the other person grow. How would you like to receive constructive criticism, both in words and the way I say them?

501    Have you ever considered that Satan might have a strategy to ruin our marriage, our family, or our children's future? What would it be? How can we recognize it more often and fight against it?

502    "Husbands, love your wives, just as Christ loved the church and gave himself up for her" (Ephesians 5:25).

TO THE WIFE: In what ways do you notice that your husband gives himself up for you?
TO THE HUSBAND: In what ways do you wish you would give yourself up for your wife more often?

*503* How do I show you dignity? How do I tear that
dignity down?

*504* What do you think are the most common forms of
manipulation in marriage? Are any of these
operating in our relationship?

*505* What do you think are warning signs that a
marriage is in jeopardy?

*506* *The Bible is like a telescope. If a man looks through his
telescope, then he sees worlds beyond; but if he looks at
his telescope, then he does not see anything but that.
The Bible is a thing to be looked through, to see that
which is beyond; but most people only look at it; and so
they see only the dead letter.*—PHILLIPS BROOKS[1]

As a couple, are we looking *through* or *at* the Bible?
How can we help each other look *through* it more
often?

*507* What would we do if one of our parents needed to
move in with us for any length of time? Let's discuss
this now—before it happens.

*508* Does sex bring us closer together, or does closeness eventually lead to sex? Do you appreciate one more than the other?

*509* What does a "fair fight" in marriage mean to you?

*510* When things don't go my way at work, how do I handle it? How about at home between us?

*511* What could I do to help you stay sexually attracted to me?

*512* *Do not pray for easy lives; pray to be stronger men. Do not pray for tasks equal to your powers; pray for the powers equal to your tasks. Then the doing of your work shall be no miracle, but you shall be a miracle. Every day you shall wonder at yourself, at the richness of life which has come to you by the grace of God.*—PHILLIPS BROOKS[2]

In our prayer life together, are we looking for the easy life—one without trouble, or do we genuinely want God's will to form our family's character, no matter what the cost?

*513* Is there anything about life in general or our current circumstances that discourages or disappoints you?

**514** *What we are is God's gift to us. What we become is our gift to God.*—LOUIS NIZER[3]

In what ways or in what areas am I reaching my fullest potential? What gifts does my life give back to God?

**515** *I have four things to learn in life:*
*To think clearly without hurry or confusion;*
*To love everybody sincerely;*
*To act in everything with the highest motives;*
*To trust in God unhesitatingly.*
—HELEN KELLER[4]

Without being too critical of yourself (try to point to more successes than failures), talk about how you're doing in each of these four areas.

**516** What do you think is the difference between emotional intimacy and physical intimacy? Which do we share more of?

**517** Doug Fields says that "men are capable of becoming more attentive and women are capable of becoming more sexually responsive."[5] Would you agree with that? How could either of these occur in our marriage?

*What does*

*a " fair fight "*

*in marriage*

*mean to you?*

*518* "'In your anger do not sin': Do not let the sun go down while you are still angry, and do not give the devil a foothold" (Ephesians 4:26-27).

What kinds of sins do we commit when we're angry (this answer may not be the same for both of us)? When are we most tempted to let the sun go down on our anger? Do we ever give the devil a foothold in our relationship?

*519* Does sex ever feel more like a duty than a pleasure? What are some ideas on how that could change?

*520* As a couple, do we tend to go around problems—or through them?

*521* Do I ever try to shift blame from myself to someone else?

*522* What kinds of "unexpected" things might I do to spice up our relationship?

523 *Spiritual maturity begins when we realize that we are God's guests in this world. We are not householders, but pilgrims; not landlords, but tenants; not owners, but guests.*—C. WILLARD FETTER[6]

In what ways are we most tempted to make this world our home too much?

524 What little or big things can I do to help make you feel that you're an extremely valuable person—to our home, to me, to the human race?

525 Think about last week. Can you remember something I said about you that was positive? Can you think of any negative words? Which kind stays with you the most?

526 Am I doing enough "warm-ups" throughout the week before I initiate sex?

527 How does it make you feel when I go two weeks or more without ever initiating sex?

*528* If you have children, the thought of taking a weekend away from them is tough, but how about four to seven days away? Write down what conditions would have to be met for you to be able to spend this much time by yourselves. Consider these points:
- How much money will we need? Where can we afford to go?
- When can we both arrange time off from work?
- What three people or families could we trust to watch our kids for that long?
- What can we tell each other so we don't feel guilty about leaving the children?

*529* Dave and Claudia Arp, columnists for *Christian Parenting Today,* talk about "chipping away at barnacles on our boat. When we did that," they said, "our marriage began to grow." Identify three small "barnacles" that are clinging to your marriage ship.

1. _____

2. _____

3. _____

Now, pick one and work on chipping it off over the next month.

530 Do you think I apologize to you easily?

531 When you think about all of our kids being grown and away from home, what are your feelings about where our marriage will be?

532 What do you think prevents couples from becoming best friends? What three things could we do to become better friends?

1. _____

2. _____

3. _____

533 Since our parenting years are actually a temporary job, what can we do in order to make sure our "retirement" from parenting has a smooth transition?

534 *Finish the Sentence . . .*
Our love life gets boring when . . .
New positions wouldn't help our sex life as much as . . .
I most want to make love to you when . . .

**535** "So they are no longer two, but one. Therefore what God has joined together, let man not separate" (Matthew 19:6).

What are some ways the world is trying to separate us in our marriage relationship?

 **536** "For this reason a man will leave his father and mother and be united to his wife, and they will become one flesh" (Genesis 2:24).

Do you ever feel that I'm more "at one" with the kids, my job, or a hobby than I am with you?

 **537** *Some pray to marry the man they love,*
*My prayer will somewhat vary:*
*I humbly pray to Heaven above*
*That I love the man I marry.*
—ROSE PASTOR STOKES, *My Prayer*[7]

In what specific ways has your love for me deepened since we first married?

As a couple,

do we tend

to go around

problems—

or through them?

538    *There are parts of a ship which taken by themselves
would sink. The engine would sink. The propeller would
sink. But when the parts of a ship are built together, they
float. So with the events of my life. Some have been
tragic. Some have been happy. But when they are built
together, they form a craft that floats and is going
someplace. And I am comforted.*—RALPH W. SOCKMAN[8]

Do you look at life that way? What are the tragic
parts and happy parts that have formed you? Are
you comforted in any way by how you've stayed
afloat through it all? How is our marriage like the
parts of a ship, working together to float to a
destination?

539    Does it ever enter your mind that there might be
"greener pastures" with someone else? At what
specific times is that thought more likely to creep
in? In what three ways could our marriage become
the "greener pastures" you sometimes think about?

1. _____

2. _____

3. _____

*540* *Ideals are like stars. You will not succeed in touching
them with your hands; but, like the seafaring man, you
choose them as your guides, and, following them, you will
reach your destiny.*—CARL SCHURZ[9]

List ten ideals in your marriage you are using as
your guide.

1. _____

2. _____

3. _____

4. _____

5. _____

6. _____

7. _____

8. _____

9. _____

10. _____

On a scale of 1 to 5 (higher number is better), rate
how well you are doing at following each of them.

*541* When I need to confront you about something, how should I go about it?
(a) Prepare me, but tell me straight out.
(b) Write me a note.
(c) Beat around the bush until I catch on.
(d) Other

How do you feel when I point out an area in your life that I think needs some growth? When should I speak up, regardless of how it might affect you emotionally?

*542* When it comes to the fruit of the Spirit, how do I measure up as they relate to our marriage on a scale of 1 (just in the beginnings of development) to 5 (well developed):
• Love
• Joy
• Peace
• Patience
• Kindness
• Goodness
• Faithfulness
• Gentleness
• Self-control

*543*    *Adultery.* What comes to your mind when you hear that word? How can we affair-proof our marriage?

*544*    What five things do you think we have to do in the next three years to start encouraging our children to own their faith (instead of borrowing ours)?

1. _____

2. _____

3. _____

4. _____

5. _____

*545*    Do I ever act as if I'm superior to you? Specifically, what do I do or say that communicates this kind of attitude? Do I act this way around other people, too? Let's think of a signal you can give me if you see me acting this way.

*546*    Do you think we are honoring God with the way we spend, give, and save our money? How could we do even better?
*Write down your approximate debts:*
*Total debt:*

*Think of three ways you can start getting out of debt:*

1. _____

2. _____

3. _____

**547** Have I done anything to lose your respect in the last five years? If so, have I totally gained back your respect? What more can I do to help this process?

**548** Come up with a family "mission statement." It doesn't have to be long, but it should be something you could display so that everyone would see it often and remember the purpose of this family.

**549** What do you think have been the major crises in our marriage? How have I handled these events? How have we handled them as a team?

**550** Being disappointed in marriage is common, since no other human can fulfill all our needs. In what way(s) are you occasionally disappointed with me? How can you handle that disappointment? What adjustments can I make to help you not feel that way too often?

*Adultery.*

*What comes to your*

*mind when you*

*hear that word?*

*How can we*

*affair-proof our*

*marriage?*

**551**  *Success is to be measured not so much by the position that one has reached in life as by the obstacles which he has overcome while trying to succeed.*—BOOKER T. WASHINGTON[10]

Is this a true statement? List the obstacles we have overcome together as a couple. In what ways are we truly successful?

**552**  *All human beings have failings, all human beings have needs and temptations and stresses. Men and women who live together through long years get to know one another's failings; but they also come to know what is worthy of respect and admiration in those they live with and in themselves. If at the end one can say, "This man used to the limit the powers that God granted him; he was worthy of love and respect and of the sacrifices of many people, made in order that he might achieve what he deemed to be his task," then that life has been lived well and there are no regrets.*—ELEANOR ROOSEVELT[11]

What have you found worthy of respect and admiration in me? Do you believe you have a task in life? What is it?

**553**  Have I broken your heart in some way in the last six months? How could I have handled that turn of events differently?

**554**  *God never gave a man a thing to do concerning which it would be irreverent to ponder how the Son of God would have done it.*—GEORGE MACDONALD[12]

If you both have the goal of honoring God in your relationship, in what ways would God have you work on your marriage to make it all that he intends for it to be?

**555**  *The rung of a ladder was never meant to rest upon, but only to hold a man's foot long enough to enable him to put the other somewhat higher.* —THOMAS HENRY HUXLEY[13]

We shouldn't put our lives into compartments. But, for a moment, examine these areas in your life together and how they enhance or hinder each other:
- spiritual
- emotional
- physical
- mental

In any of these areas, are you "resting on the rung" instead of seeking to climb higher? Write down or discuss what it would look like to move up one more rung in each area. What is an action step you can take this week to begin that process?

**556** Dave and Jan Stoop define intimacy as "the joyful union that comes when two people learn together how to give love and how to accept love".[14] What do you think about this definition?

**557** On a scale of 1 to 10 (10 being greater), rate these potential barriers to intimacy in your marriage:

HIS     HERS
_____   _____ selfishness
_____   _____ poor parental example
_____   _____ unresolved issues from childhood
_____   _____ unresolved issues from the marriage
_____   _____ guilt
_____   _____ our busy schedule
_____   _____ wrong expectations of my mate
_____   _____ differing sexual needs
_____   _____ not having much in common
_____   _____ familiarity
_____   _____ my introverted/extroverted personality
_____   _____ the way we resolve conflict

What one area can we start working on in the next month? Where do we start?

558  What past marital mistakes have I made that you
believe I haven't apologized for (if any)? What is it
about these particular mistakes that are hard for
you to forget?

559  "Marriage should be honored by all, and the
marriage bed kept pure, for God will judge the
adulterer and all the sexually immoral"
(Hebrews 13:4).

The second part of this verse is widely accepted
and understood, but the first often goes ignored.
What does it mean to "honor" marriage? Is this
happening with you? What two things can you do to
ensure that you are honoring it more than you did
last year?

1. _____

2. _____

560  Read the Song of Solomon in the next week and
talk about what it meant when it was written and
what it means to your marriage today.

*561* "But since there is so much immorality, each man should have his own wife, and each woman her own husband. The husband should fulfill his marital duty to his wife, and likewise the wife to her husband. The wife's body does not belong to her alone but also to her husband. In the same way, the husband's body does not belong to him alone but also to his wife. Do not deprive each other except by mutual consent and for a time, so that you may devote yourselves to prayer. Then come together again so that Satan will not tempt you because of your lack of self-control" (1 Corinthians 7:2-5).

What is the reason Paul gives for marriage? What "duty" is Paul referring to?

Tim LaHaye says that "when one marries, he forfeits control of his body to the one he marries."[15] Is that true? Has it been true for us? Should it be more true?

What is your definition of "deprive"? How does this intentionally or unintentionally happen in our marriage?

Paul seems sure that Satan will tempt us if we don't come back together. How does he tempt you?

*Can our children trust*

*us enough to look to us*

*for learning the big*

*lessons of life?*

**562** What are ten ways we can divorce-proof our marriage?

1. _____

2. _____

3. _____

4. _____

5. _____

6. _____

7. _____

8. _____

9. _____

10. _____

 **563** *People are lonely because they build walls instead of bridges.*—JOSEPH FORT NEWTON[16]

In what three ways do I build bridges to you and others?

1. _____

2. _____

3. _____

In what three ways do I build walls around myself to keep people away?

1. _____

2. _____

3. _____

564 In what ways can I challenge you spiritually to "excel still more" without nagging, making you feel inadequate, or making you feel that I'm trying to get you "up to my level"?

565 Name ten things you think I'm really good at:

1. _____

2. _____

3. _____

4. _____

5. _____

6. _____

7. _____

8. _____

9. _____

10. _____

*566* Complete this sentence in five different ways (serious and/or funny):

When you_____,

I feel_____.

*567* Try to name at least five different nights out you've never taken before (i.e., an opera, a play, a hockey game, eating dinner on the roof). Choose one you both agree would be interesting, and within the next week, put that activity into your schedule.

1. _____

2. _____

3. _____

4. _____

5. _____

*568* *A man has made at least a start on discovering the meaning of human life when he plants shade trees under which he knows full well he will never sit.*
—ELTON TRUEBLOOD[17]

Besides our children, who are we investing our lives in? Is there a local organization in which we could get involved?

*569* Each of you think of ten reasons (serious or lighthearted) you love the other. Enter these below after you're done.

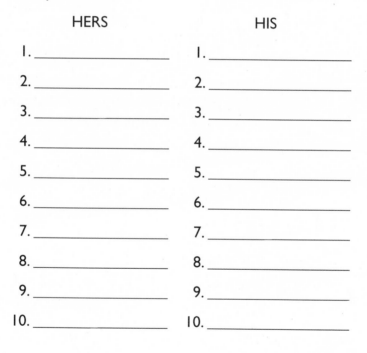

| HERS | HIS |
|------|-----|
| 1. _____ | 1. _____ |
| 2. _____ | 2. _____ |
| 3. _____ | 3. _____ |
| 4. _____ | 4. _____ |
| 5. _____ | 5. _____ |
| 6. _____ | 6. _____ |
| 7. _____ | 7. _____ |
| 8. _____ | 8. _____ |
| 9. _____ | 9. _____ |
| 10. _____ | 10. _____ |

*570* Fear imprisons, faith liberates; fear paralyzes, faith empowers; fear disheartens, faith encourages; fear sickens, faith heals; fear makes useless, faith makes serviceable—and, most of all, fear puts hopelessness at the heart of life, while faith rejoices in its God.
—HARRY EMERSON FOSDICK[18]

Using this quote as a measuring stick, in what ways are you a fearful person? a faithful person?

*571* Peace is a big theme in the Bible, yet with the pace of most families—and the pressures they face— peace is often elusive. What are three things you could do so that your marriage and family are able to experience more peace "on the outside"?

1. _____

2. _____

3. _____

What are three ways you can start experiencing more peace on the inside?

1. _____

2. _____

3. _____

*572* Focusing on the positive things about your mate isn't as easy as concentrating on the negative—but you need to do it anyway! Each of you talk about the positive things you see in these areas:
• achievements
• service to God and others
• special talents and skills
• character qualities
• child rearing

*573* Write down some of the ways in which you've tried to stimulate growth in your relationship, but then have quit because of laziness or "toobusyitis." You started some of these things with good motives, but they just weren't right at the time. That doesn't mean they were bad ideas. Which one of these could you start again with a renewed vision for what it was meant to accomplish?

*574* In *60 One-Minute Marriage Builders,* Dave and Claudia Arp talk about giving each other "marriage vitamins" to build the other person up. Each of you think of five different "vitamins" you would like to receive from your mate.

# *We're Finally Alone . . .*

| For Her | For Him |
|---|---|
| 1. _____ | 1. _____ |
| 2. _____ | 2. _____ |
| 3. _____ | 3. _____ |
| 4. _____ | 4. _____ |
| 5. _____ | 5. _____ |

*575*   *All a child's life depends on the ideal it has of its parents. Destroy that and everything goes—morals, behavior, everything. Absolute trust in someone else is the essence of education.*—E. M. FORSTER[19]

Are we up for this challenge? Can our children trust us enough to look to us for learning the big lessons of life? What are the five most important lessons they should be learning? How can we teach them these lessons?

1. _____

2. _____

3. _____

4. _____

5. _____

# Twelve Rules for Happiness

Here are a few ways to get the most out of the following "rules":
- Rate your marriage team on how well you're doing.
- Rate yourself or (if you dare) each other on where you think you are.
- Develop a mini-plan on how to get closer to these ideals.

**1. Live a simple life.** Be temperate in your habits. Avoid self-seeking and selfishness. Make simplicity the keynote of your daily plans. Simple things are best.

**2. Spend less than you earn.** This may be difficult, but it pays big dividends. Keep out of debt. Cultivate frugality, prudence, and self-denial. Avoid extravagance.

**3. Think constructively.** Train yourself to think clearly and accurately. Store your mind with useful thoughts. Stand porter at the door of your mind.

**4. Cultivate a yielding disposition.** Resist the common tendency to want things your own way. Try to see the other person's point of view.

**5. Be grateful.** Begin the day with gratitude for your opportunities and blessings. Be glad for the privilege of life and work.

**6. Rule your moods.** Cultivate a mental attitude of peace and good will.

**7. Give generously.** There is no greater joy in life than to render happiness to others by means of intelligent giving.

**8. Work with right motives.** The highest purpose of your life should be to grow in spiritual grace and power.

**9. Be interested in others.** Direct your mind away from yourself. In the degree that you give, serve, and help will you experience the by-product of happiness.

**10. Live in a daylight compartment.** This means living one day at a time. Concentrate on your immediate task. Make the most of today for it is all you have.

**11. Have a hobby.** Nature study, walking, gardening, music, golfing, carpentry, stamp collecting, sketching, foreign language, books, photography, social service, public speaking, travel, authorship are samples. Cultivate an avocation to which you can turn for diversion and relaxation.

**12. Keep up your relationship with God.** True and enduring happiness depends on close alliance with him. It is your privilege to share his thoughts for your spiritual nourishment, and to have a constant assurance of divine protection and guidance.

National Religious Press[1]

# ENDNOTES

## Level One

1. Doug Fields, *365 Things Every Couple Should Know* (Eugene, Oreg.: Harvest House Publishers, 1993).

## Level Two

1. *The Pocket Book of Quotations,* (New York: Simon & Schuster, 1942, 1952).
2. Doug Fields, *365 Things Every Couple Should Know* (Eugene, Oreg.: Harvest House Publishers, 1993).
3. Charles L. Wallis, ed., *The Treasure Chest* (New York: Harper & Row Publishers, 1965).
4. Fields, *365 Things.*

## Level Three

1. Charles L. Wallis, ed., *The Treasure Chest* (New York: Harper & Row Publishers, 1965).
2. Wallis, *Treasure Chest.*
3. *The Pocket Book of Quotations,* (New York: Simon & Schuster, 1942, 1952).
4. Doug Fields, *365 Things Every Couple Should Know* (Eugene, Oreg.: Harvest House Publishers, 1993).
5. Wallis, *Treasure Chest.*

## Level Four

1. Charles L. Wallis, ed., *The Treasure Chest* (New York: Harper & Row Publishers, 1965).
2. Wallis, *Treasure Chest.*
3. Wallis, *Treasure Chest.*
4. Wallis, *Treasure Chest.*
5. Wallis, *Treasure Chest.*
6. Wallis, *Treasure Chest.*
7. Wallis, *Treasure Chest.*
8. Wallis, *Treasure Chest.*
9. Wallis, *Treasure Chest.*

10. Wallis, *Treasure Chest*.
11. *The Pocket Book of Quotations*, (New York: Simon & Schuster, 1942, 1952).
12. *Pocket Book of Quotations*.

Level Five
1. Charles L. Wallis, ed., *The Treasure Chest* (New York: Harper & Row Publishers, 1965).
2. Wallis, *Treasure Chest*.
3. Wallis, *Treasure Chest*.
4. Wallis, *Treasure Chest*.
5. Doug Fields, *365 Things Every Couple Should Know* (Eugene, Oreg.: Harvest House Publishers, 1993).
6. Wallis, *Treasure Chest*.
7. *The Pocket Book of Quotations*, (New York: Simon & Schuster, 1942, 1952).
8. Wallis, *Treasure Chest*.
9. Wallis, *Treasure Chest*.
10. Wallis, *Treasure Chest*.
11. Wallis, *Treasure Chest*.
12. Wallis, *Treasure Chest*.
13. Wallis, *Treasure Chest*.
14. Dave Stoop and Jan Stoop, *The Intimacy Factor* (Nashville, Tenn.: Thomas Nelson Publishers, 1993).
15. Tim LaHaye and Beverly LaHaye, *The Act of Marriage* (Grand Rapids, Mich.: Zondervan Publishing House, 1976).
16. Wallis, *Treasure Chest*.
17. Wallis, *Treasure Chest*.
18. Wallis, *Treasure Chest*.
19. Wallis, *Treasure Chest*.

Twelve Rules for Happiness
1. Charles L. Wallis, ed., *The Treasure Chest* (New York: Harper & Row Publishers, 1965).

# INDEX

You may wish to look up questions under a particular topic rather than going through the book randomly or in numerical order. For questions by topic, use this simple index. Many questions appear in more than one category.

## Communication

## Dreams and Wishes

# We're Finally Alone...

## Family and Parenting

| | | | | | |
|---|---|---|---|---|---|
| 142 | 260 | 298 | 365 | 421 | 494 |
| 153 | 268 | 303 | 371 | 427 | 496 |
| 154 | 270 | 305 | 385 | 429 | 507 |
| 160 | 274 | 307 | 391 | 431 | 528 |
| 162 | 277 | 308 | 399 | 444 | 531 |
| 168 | 278 | 309 | 403 | 447 | 533 |
| 183 | 279 | 310 | 405 | 454 | 536 |
| 209 | 282 | 329 | 406 | 457 | 544 |
| 211 | 287 | 337 | 410 | 469 | 546 |
| 223 | 290 | 349 | 411 | 480 | 548 |
| 231 | 293 | 361 | 413 | 492 | 571 |
| 244 | 294 | 363 | 418 | 493 | 575 |
| 255 | | | | | |

## Getting Honest

| | | | | | |
|---|---|---|---|---|---|
| 133 | 207 | 270 | 340 | 433 | 500 |
| 140 | 222 | 275 | 356 | 448 | 505 |
| 142 | 226 | 291 | 357 | 453 | 510 |
| 148 | 227 | 296 | 369 | 458 | 521 |
| 149 | 232 | 305 | 373 | 461 | 536 |
| 152 | 234 | 306 | 378 | 463 | 539 |
| 156 | 235 | 308 | 383 | 465 | 541 |
| 158 | 238 | 309 | 384 | 478 | 543 |
| 165 | 239 | 313 | 386 | 481 | 545 |
| 169 | 246 | 320 | 387 | 484 | 547 |
| 172 | 247 | 323 | 407 | 487 | 550 |
| 177 | 262 | 326 | 414 | 488 | 553 |
| 179 | 263 | 329 | 424 | 489 | 558 |
| 189 | 264 | 339 | 431 | 495 | |

## Getting to Know You

## Helping Each Other Grow

## We're Finally Alone...

### Personal Opinions

| | | | | | |
|---|---|---|---|---|---|
| 105 | 159 | 241 | 302 | 409 | 504 |
| 121 | 164 | 249 | 331 | 467 | 505 |
| 131 | 186 | 252 | 369 | 479 | 538 |
| 138 | 210 | 259 | 382 | 482 | 556 |
| 150 | 214 | 273 | 393 | 497 | 559 |
| 158 | 221 | 285 | 394 | 499 | |

### Remember and Reminisce

| | | | | | |
|---|---|---|---|---|---|
| 100 | 122 | 167 | 218 | 267 | 345 |
| 102 | 140 | 168 | 229 | 268 | 346 |
| 107 | 145 | 174 | 230 | 291 | 351 |
| 110 | 153 | 176 | 253 | 301 | 468 |
| 118 | 154 | 180 | 254 | 316 | |

### Sex and Romance

| | | | | | |
|---|---|---|---|---|---|
| 104 | 184 | 314 | 393 | 475 | 534 |
| 112 | 191 | 318 | 396 | 476 | 537 |
| 113 | 196 | 333 | 428 | 482 | 539 |
| 117 | 212 | 336 | 432 | 483 | 543 |
| 123 | 217 | 338 | 438 | 486 | 553 |
| 132 | 225 | 348 | 440 | 489 | 555 |
| 141 | 236 | 351 | 445 | 508 | 557 |
| 144 | 237 | 354 | 447 | 511 | 560 |
| 151 | 243 | 362 | 448 | 516 | 561 |
| 165 | 244 | 367 | 450 | 517 | 567 |
| 170 | 245 | 380 | 461 | 519 | 569 |
| 171 | 265 | 382 | 462 | 522 | |
| 178 | 280 | 385 | 471 | 526 | |
| 180 | 301 | 388 | 473 | 527 | |
| 181 | 312 | 390 | 474 | 528 | |

## Spiritual Life

| | | | | | |
|---|---|---|---|---|---|
| 105 | 250 | 321 | 385 | 447 | 542 |
| 115 | 256 | 324 | 389 | 452 | 544 |
| 121 | 266 | 327 | 391 | 466 | 548 |
| 130 | 269 | 328 | 394 | 470 | 554 |
| 160 | 276 | 342 | 404 | 472 | 555 |
| 173 | 281 | 350 | 408 | 491 | 559 |
| 203 | 283 | 352 | 420 | 501 | 561 |
| 205 | 284 | 353 | 431 | 502 | 563 |
| 213 | 295 | 366 | 434 | 506 | 564 |
| 219 | 297 | 372 | 436 | 512 | 568 |
| 220 | 298 | 375 | 438 | 514 | 570 |
| 242 | 311 | 376 | 442 | 518 | 571 |
| 246 | 317 | 381 | 446 | 523 | 572 |

## Troubles and Struggles

| | | | | | |
|---|---|---|---|---|---|
| 134 | 299 | 359 | 431 | 459 | 538 |
| 138 | 300 | 363 | 434 | 468 | 543 |
| 208 | 306 | 364 | 435 | 478 | 547 |
| 209 | 308 | 372 | 436 | 484 | 549 |
| 228 | 325 | 374 | 437 | 492 | 550 |
| 233 | 327 | 399 | 439 | 493 | 551 |
| 246 | 334 | 400 | 441 | 509 | 553 |
| 272 | 335 | 419 | 448 | 513 | 558 |
| 286 | 341 | 423 | 450 | 520 | 562 |
| 294 | 354 | 427 | 455 | 535 | |

# We're Finally Alone . . .

## Working on Marriage

| | | | | | |
|---|---|---|---|---|---|
| 130 | 283 | 376 | 437 | 493 | 547 |
| 139 | 297 | 380 | 438 | 499 | 549 |
| 170 | 299 | 382 | 439 | 504 | 550 |
| 179 | 308 | 387 | 440 | 505 | 551 |
| 204 | 312 | 388 | 441 | 509 | 553 |
| 207 | 315 | 399 | 448 | 518 | 554 |
| 208 | 317 | 401 | 450 | 520 | 555 |
| 217 | 319 | 404 | 451 | 522 | 561 |
| 224 | 325 | 412 | 454 | 529 | 562 |
| 228 | 329 | 423 | 455 | 530 | 571 |
| 231 | 331 | 426 | 459 | 532 | 572 |
| 238 | 338 | 427 | 464 | 535 | 573 |
| 244 | 340 | 428 | 475 | 536 | 574 |
| 263 | 356 | 430 | 476 | 537 | |
| 265 | 358 | 431 | 478 | 539 | |
| 271 | 364 | 433 | 484 | 540 | |

# ADDITIONAL RESOURCES
# ON MARRIAGE

Allender, Dan B., and Tremper Longman III. *Intimate Allies: Rediscovering God's Design for Marriage and Becoming Soul Mates for Life.* Wheaton, Ill.: Tyndale House, 1995.

Crabb, Lawrence J. *The Marriage Builder.* Grand Rapids: Zondervan, 1992.

Fields, Doug. *Creative Romance.* Eugene, Oreg.: Harvest House, 1991.

Griffith, Harry, and Emily Griffith. *This Love We Share: Daily Devotions to Bring Wholeness to Your Marriage.* Wheaton, Ill.: Tyndale House, 1995.

Harley, Willard. *His Needs, Her Needs.* Grand Rapids: Fleming H. Revell, 1986.

Hybels, Bill. *Fit to Be Tied: Making Marriage Last a Lifetime.* New York: HarperCollins, 1994.

Jenkins, Jerry B. *Still the One: Loving Thoughts from a Devoted Spouse.* Colorado Springs: Focus on the Family, 1995.

Johnson, Greg, and Mike Yorkey. *The Second Decade of Love.* Wheaton, Ill.: Tyndale House, 1994.

Rainey, Dennis, and Barbara Rainey. *The New Building Your Mate's Self-Esteem.* Nashville: Nelson, 1995.

Smalley, Gary. *Crazy in Love.* Irving, Tex.: Word, 1996.

Smalley, Gary, and John Trent. *The Language of Love.* New York: Pocket Books, 1992.

Warren, Neil Clark. *The Triumphant Marriage.* Colorado Springs: Focus on the Family, 1994.

Wheat, Ed. *Love Life for Every Married Couple.* New York: HarperCollins, 1991.

# We're Finally Alone...

Wright, H. Norman. *Communication: Key to Your Marriage.* Ventura, Calif.: Regal, 1995.

Yagel, Bobbie, and Myron Yagel. *15 Minutes to Build a Stronger Marriage: Weekly Togetherness for Busy Couples.* Wheaton, Ill.: Tyndale House, 1995.

Young, Ed. *Romancing the Home: How to Have a Marriage That Sizzles.* Nashville: Broadman and Holman, 1993.